TRUE OF
FALSE?

ILOVEYOU - Message (Rich Text)

File Edit View Insert Format PGP Tools Actions Help

Reply | Reply to All | Forward

From: UK Help Desk
To: Sharaz Afgan
Cc:
Subject: ILOVEYOU

LOVE-LETTER-FOR-Y
OU.TXT.vbs

If you open this e-mail,
you're likely to:

a) get a date.

b) find a cheesy
Valentine from your mom.

c) catch a nasty
computer virus.

ANSWER: C

You're likely to catch a nasty computer virus!

In 2000, the ILOVEYOU virus—or "Love Bug"— traveled through cyberspace as an attachment to e-mail messages. When recipients opened the attachment, the virus was loaded onto their hard drives. It erased their music, photos, and other files. Then it broke into their address books and sent copies of itself to their friends.

Before it was stopped, the Love Bug infected millions of computers.

Find out more about who's threatening your computer—and who's trying to protect it.

Book design Red Herring Design/NYC

Library of Congress Cataloging-in-Publication Data
Newman, Matthew. 1955–
You have mail : true stories of cybercrime / by Matthew Newman.
p. cm. — 24/7 : science behind the scenes
Includes bibliographical references and index.
ISBN-13: 978-0-531-12085-9 (lib. bdg.)   978-0-531-18731-9 (pbk.)
ISBN-10: 0-531-12085-6 (lib. bdg.)   0-531-18731-4 (pbk.)
1. Computer security—Juvenile literature. 2. Computer crimes—Juvenile literature. I. Title.
QA76.9.A25N49 2007
005.8—dc22   2006021233

Published simultaneously in Canada. Printed in the United States of America.

SCHOLASTIC, FRANKLIN WATTS, and associated logos are trademarks and/or registered trademarks of Scholastic Inc.
1 2 3 4 5 6 7 8 9 10 R 17 16 15 14 13 12 11 10 09 08

LOVELETTER.txt - WordPad

File Edit View Insert Format Help

Date: 04/05/2000 3:29:02 PM

YOU HAVE MAIL

Subject:

To:

kindly ch   LOVELETT

rem barok -loveletter(vbe) <i hate go

rem   by   yder / ispyder@n

On Error Res

dim fso

True Stories of Cybercrime

Matthew Newman

WARNING: Beware. You're about to meet some dangerous cybercrooks. Some cause trouble by breaking into other people's computers. Others are identity thieves who steal personal information such as credit card numbers. And some are terrorists who use the Internet to plan attacks.

Franklin Watts
An Imprint of Scholastic Inc.
New York • Toronto • London • Auckland • Sydney
Mexico City • New Delhi • Hong Kong
Danbury, Connecticut

CONTENTS

4

Real stories about people who are using the Internet for good—and for evil.

Could hackers use the Internet to cause chaos?

A teenager's prank causes problems around the world.

This woman is spying on terrorists online.

CYBERCRIME DOWNLOAD

Here's more about cybercrooks and their nasty scams.

There's a war being fought on the Internet.

On one side are the crooks and terrorists who use it for illegal activities.

CYBERCRIME 411

On the other side are the computer whizzes and crime fighters who want to bring them down.

How is this war being fought? And who's winning it?

IN THIS SECTION:

- ▶ how computers turn into zombies;
- ▶ why White Hats don't like Black Hats;
- ▶ and how Black Hats go about their dirty work.

Cyberspeak

Cybercrooks and the people who track them have their own way of speaking. Find out what their vocabulary means.

The cops released the **hacker** who broke into our company network. They said she did it just to show that we need a better **firewall**.

hacker
(HAK-ur) a skilled programmer who breaks into computer networks. Some do it for fun or to test how secure those systems are. Others, sometimes called crackers, have criminal motives. This book uses the term *hacker* for anyone who invades computer systems—whether their motives are good or bad.

firewall
(FYRE-wahl) an electronic barrier that keeps out hackers

If a **virus** gets into our computers, we could lose a lot of important data.

virus
(VYE-rus) a destructive program that infects people's computers without their knowledge. It spreads by attaching itself to e-mails or files that are sent from one computer to another.

Isn't he the hacker who created the worm that infected computers all around the world last year?

worm
(wurm) a nasty program that slows or shuts down computers. It spreads quickly through networks by copying itself again and again.

An act of cyberterrorism could cause a major blackout.

cyberterrorism
(SYE-bur-TAIR-ur-izm) an attack on the computer networks that control power plants and other large systems

Say What?

Here's more cyberlingo.

script kiddie
(skript KID-ee) an inexperienced or unskilled hacker who uses programs written by someone else to break into computer systems
*"Hackers look down on **script kiddies**."*

Trojan horse
(TRO-jun hors) a program that looks like useful software but really contains a virus or other harmful program
*"The free online game was really a **Trojan horse**, and the virus hidden inside it damaged his system."*

zombies
(ZOM-beez) computers that have been taken over by hackers. The hackers can control zombies without the computer owners' knowledge.
*"They used a lot of **zombies** to attack their target."*

Black Hats
Versus
White Hats

Black Hats are hackers who are up to no good. And White Hats are hackers who want to make the virtual world a safer place.

BEWARE THE BLACK HATS

Black Hat File #1:
Super Hackers

WHO ARE THEY?
Super hackers, or crackers, are highly skilled troublemakers. They like to show off their programming skills by breaking into computer networks. Many design nasty worms and viruses that can seriously damage any computers they infect.

WHY ARE THEY ON THE WEB?
Most super hackers spend much of their time online. Computers are their whole world. But they don't like the Internet's rules. They break them by hacking into computer networks. They want to show that they can outsmart the **software** designers at companies like Microsoft.

Black Hat File #2:
Identity Thieves

WHO ARE THEY?
Identity thieves run scams to steal people's **Social Security** numbers, bank account numbers, and other personal information. Most identity thieves work for organized crime groups. Many experts say that they are a bigger threat than cyberterrorists.

WHY ARE THEY ON THE WEB?
Identity thieves send out fake e-mail offers designed to trick people into giving them personal information such as passwords and driver's license numbers. That's called **phishing** (see page 50 to learn more about phishing). Or they get that information by hacking into people's computers.

They use those stolen identities to get credit cards. Or sometimes they can steal directly from someone's bank account. They can also use people's e-mail accounts to reach other potential victims.

Black Hat File #3:
Cyberterrorists

WHO ARE THEY?
They could belong to an international **terrorist** group like **Al Qaeda**. U.S. officials also believe that Iran, North Korea, Russia, and China have trained hackers to engage in Internet warfare.

WHY ARE THEY ON THE WEB?
Many terrorists use the Internet to raise money, recruit others, and share information about their plans. But the term *cyberterrorist* really applies to those who plot to attack computer networks. A large-scale **cyberattack** could affect power plants, transportation systems, and even the water supply. No such attack has ever taken place, and most experts think a major cyberattack is unlikely.

HOW MANY ARE OUT THERE?
There's been a dramatic explosion in the number of Web sites operated by terrorist organizations. According to estimates, there were just 12 in 1998. By 2006, there were more than 4,800 sites operated by terrorists.

WHO'S TRACKING THEM?
Rita Katz formed a company called SITE—Search for International Terrorist Entities—to track terrorists on the Net. She slips into terrorist chat rooms and listens to their plots. Read Katz's story on page 37.

11

FAMOUS BLACK HATS
Here's a look at some of the Web's most notorious hackers.

Robert Morris
In 1988, Cornell University student Robert Morris released the first worm into the Internet. It made copies of itself faster than he expected, and caused computers around the country to **crash**. Today, he teaches at MIT.

Kevin Mitnick
Kevin Mitnick began hacking as a teenager. He became skilled at breaking into corporate computer systems and stealing their secrets. Mitnick developed a reputation as a dangerous cybercriminal. But he claims he did it for the thrill—not the money.

In 1995, Mitnick was arrested and sent to prison for five years. Some people thought his punishment was too harsh. He's still hacking today, but he has switched hats. Now he shows companies how to protect themselves from young Kevin Mitnicks.

Legion of Doom
The Legion of Doom was the name of a group of hackers in the 1980s and 1990s. LOD hacked into **infrastructure** systems such as phone networks. But the group generally didn't cause much damage. Mostly they wanted to show people how vulnerable the Internet was to attack. LOD members used comic book names such as Lex Luthor, Bloodaxe, and Phiber Optik.

Sven Jaschan
This young hacker created a dangerous worm called Sasser. Turn to page 27 to read about the trouble it caused around the world.

WHITE HATS TO THE RESCUE

White Hat File #1:
Sneakers

WHO ARE THEY?
Sneakers are hackers hired by companies to test the security of their Web sites and computer networks. Then they fix any problems they find.

WHAT DO THEY DO?
Sneakers try to break into a company's system without anyone knowing. If they succeed, that means that other people can, too. Groups of sneakers are called **tiger teams**. The 1992 film *Sneakers* was about a tiger team that defined its job this way: "To break into people's places to make sure that no one can break into their places."

White Hat File #2:
Honeypots

WHAT ARE THEY?
Honeypots are traps set by White Hats to catch Black Hats.

HOW DO THEY WORK?
A honeypot appears to be regular computer. But it is actually connected to a White Hat's computer. The White Hat has left holes in its security system to make it inviting to hackers. He wants hackers to take the bait and break into it.

Once hackers attack a honeypot, White Hats can spy on them online to find out about their hacking techniques. That information helps White Hats to design new ways to protect computer networks.

FAMOUS WHITE HATS

Here's a look at some brainiacs under those white hats.

Gordon Lynn

Lynn, who goes by the nickname "Fyodor," has used honeypots to catch many Black Hats. He describes himself this way: "I am a hacker. The good kind. I enjoy tinkering with computers, exploring networks, pushing hardware and software to its limits."

Tsutomu Shimomura

Tsutomu Shimomura (*below right*) helped catch the computer outlaw Kevin Mitnick. In 1994, Mitnick made the mistake of stealing software and e-mail from Shimomura's computer. Shimomura helped track him down, and two months later Mitnick was caught. Shimomura's story became a book and a movie—both called *Takedown*.

HACKER FOR HIRE

These days, everyone wants to hire White Hats. Here's a look at just a few places that keep them on the payroll.

Employer #1: U.S. Government

▶ The Department of Homeland Security (**DHS**) has its own National CyberSecurity Division to monitor cyberterrorist threats.

▶ The Central Intelligence Agency (**CIA**) has a branch called the Information Operations Center. It evaluates threats to U.S. computer systems from foreign governments, criminal organizations, and hackers.

▶ The Federal Bureau of Investigation (**FBI**) tracks cybercriminals—from hackers to mobsters.

Employer #2: Security Firms

There are thousands of private security firms that sell their services to everyone from big businesses to small home computer users.

Employer #3: Software Giants

Big software companies like Microsoft are often targets of hack attacks. That's why they have in-house experts to patch their systems when hackers punch holes in them. They also track down the cyberintruders. The Microsoft Security Response Center (MSRC) is a SWAT team of super programmers who sniff out hack threats.

TRUE-LIFE CASE FILES!

24 hours a day, 7 days a week, 365 days a year, criminals are up to no good on the Internet. But there are many computer experts working around the clock to stop them.

IN THIS SECTION:

▶ who the Internet's bad guys are and what they're doing;

▶ how one teenager caused problems for millions of computer users;

▶ can a cyberspy stop terrorists?

24/7 Pop Quiz

Take a second and test your cybercrime IQ.

1 You know your computer has been infected by a virus if

a) it starts overheating.
b) some of your files are suddenly missing.
c) it takes a sick day.

2 A hacker is

a) someone with a bad cough.
b) a terrorist planning an attack on the Internet.
c) a skilled programmer who can break into computer networks.

3 A White Hat's goal is to

a) protect the Internet from attacks.
b) create a global community of hackers.
c) make a fashion statement.

4 Sneakers are computer experts who

a) sneak up on Black Hats while they're hacking.
b) wear running shoes to work.
c) break into computer networks so they can find their weak points.

5 Legion of Doom is the name of

a) a popular, but illegal, computer game.
b) a group of hackers active in the 1980s and 1990s.
c) software developed to bypass honeypots.

Answers: 1–b; 2–c; 3–a; 4–c; 5–b.

The World
21st Century

The Rise of Cybercrime

The threat from cybercriminals is growing. Just how dangerous are they?

Surprise Attack

Could terrorists use the Web as a weapon?

It starts with a blackout. Without warning, all the lights go out in New York and Los Angeles. Then, cities across the country—Philadelphia, Chicago, Dallas, Las Vegas—are plunged into darkness.

On August 14, 2003, millions of people in North America lost their electricity. People in Detroit, Toronto, New York City, and the surrounding areas were in the dark. In 2005, the CIA held a drill to imagine an even worse scenario.

With the power out, communication networks begin to fail. Computers, phones, and TVs stop working. Transportation comes to a stop. Businesses are forced to close. Police and fire departments can't get through the traffic jams. There's confusion everywhere.

In the air, navigation systems have failed. Emergency communication systems are overwhelmed. Pilots can't contact control towers for instructions. They don't know where or when to land.

This is a picture of America under attack. Terrorists are causing panic throughout the nation. But this is not like any previous terrorist attack.

It's a cyberattack.

In 2005, the CIA held a secret, three-day drill. It was called Silent Horizon. During this exercise, the intelligence agency examined threats to major U.S. computer systems. Could terrorists really knock out power in major U.S. cities?

Actually, it's a pretend cyberattack. It's part of a cyber war game played out by the CIA in a secret location in 2005.

There's a new bunch of bad guys out there—cyberterrorists—and the United States government is preparing to fight them. So CIA computer experts go through hundreds of possible attack **scenarios**. They play war games to help them figure out all the different ways that terrorists could turn computers against the country.

But is it really possible for terrorists to use the Internet as a weapon? Could they invade important computer networks? And if they did, could they do a lot of damage?

Agents from the Department of Homeland Security take part in the 2006 "Cyber Storm" war games. These agents were testing how they'd respond to attacks on the Internet.

How Worried Should We Be?

Experts disagree on how real the threat is.

Even before the attacks of September 11, 2001, the government warned that terrorists might try to attack U.S. infrastructure systems. Those are the basic services needed to make communities work. They include transportation and communication, as well as water and electricity.

By attacking the computer networks that control those systems, terrorist hackers could cause great chaos.

The FBI believes that the threat of such an attack is rapidly growing. U.S. Congressman Adam Putnam of Florida agrees. He's a leader on cybersecurity issues. Putnam says that the U.S. has left "our cyber-backdoor wide open" to attacks from terrorist groups.

But many other experts believe that a major cyberattack is highly unlikely. They say that terrorist groups don't have the **expertise** to it pull off.

"Cyberterrorism is just not at the top of the list of things to worry about," says Dennis

U.S. Congressman Adam Putnam from Florida argued that the threat of cyberterrorism is very real.

McGrath from Dartmouth College.

In fact, there are many safeguards that protect against a massive attack on U.S. infrastructure. For example, the nationwide electrical system is made up of over 3,000 power companies. And they each have backup systems. Terrorists would need to be highly organized to attack all of them at the same time.

An electronic board shows how power is distributed throughout California. Computer security experts work to make sure that the networks controlling important infrastructure systems can't be invaded by cyberterrorists.

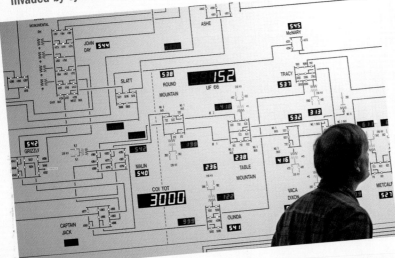

The Legion of Doom hackers were active in the 1980s and 1990s. They took their name from comic book villains. It is not clear what members of the group are doing now.

Young Invaders

Hackers have been breaking into computers for years.

So why is there so much concern about cyberattacks? It's probably because hackers have been breaking into computer networks for the past 20 years. Many of these hackers are young—and aren't launching attacks. Still, they've shown that the Internet can be at risk.

Here are just a few examples of break-ins by computer hackers.

In 1989, hackers calling themselves the Legion of Doom took over the BellSouth telephone system. They **tapped** phone lines and rerouted calls.

In 1997, a hacker shut down the computer system of an airport control tower in Massachusetts. He was caught before any terrible accidents occurred.

23

And in 1998, Russian hackers got into Pentagon computers and **downloaded** thousands of sensitive files. They were never caught.

In 2005 alone, hackers caused an estimated $15 billion in damage. And the number of attacks goes up every year. There were 250 cyberattacks during the first six months of 2006. That was 50 percent more than during the same period the year before.

Still, none of these attacks were launched by terrorists. Most experts say that terrorists don't yet have the hacking skills needed to wage cyberwar. They believe it's unlikely that terrorists could ever launch an assault that would cripple the country.

But the government isn't taking any chances. It treats cyberterrorism as seriously as any other threat against homeland security. New defenses are put in place all the time. The government, along with private industry, is spending billions to make sure that the CIA's war game scenarios never become a reality.

Rise of the Cybercrooks

A crime wave hits Web surfers.

The possibility of cyberterrorism is frightening. But there's another Internet threat that's already affecting millions of people. It's called cybercrime, and it's on the rise.

Every day, Internet users are plagued by **spam** and junk e-mail, worms, and viruses. They are also targeted by phishers. These are identity thieves who use fake e-mail offers and phony Web sites to steal people's personal information. They try to get their hands on bank account information, Social Security numbers, passwords, and other data.

Using that information, they get new credit cards and go on Internet shopping sprees. Or they commit many other kinds of crimes.

Some crooks steal many identities at once. They break into databases where large companies keep information about their clients. According to *USA Today*, at least 130

Cybercrooks want *you!* Never give out important personal information such as usernames, passwords, or banking information. And don't open strange e-mails—no matter how tempting they look!

major database break-ins took place in 2005. Those break-ins put more than 55 million people at risk of identity theft.

Still, the Internet isn't always risky—especially if users are careful. Firewalls and other security software can protect computers. So can common sense. "There are parts of your city that you wouldn't walk through late at night," says Ron Tarney of the CyberSecurity Industry Alliance. "The Internet is the same way. Know the safe places to go." 24/7

In the next case, find out about a teenager who launched a major attack on the Web.

Waffensen, Germany
April 30, 2004

The Lone Hacker

Could one teenager in his basement create chaos around the world?

DENMARK

Baltic Sea

Flensburg

North Sea

Kiel

Neustadt

Stralsun

Fehmarn

Cuxhaven

Lübeck

Rostock

Wismar

Wilhelms-haven

Bremer-haven

Schwerin

Neubranden

Oldenburg

Bremen

Hamburg

Ludwigslust

Waffensen

Elbe

Perleberg

Oranienb

Stendal

Berlin

Potsdam

annover

Brandenburg

Braunschweig

Magdeburg

Bernburg

Dessau

Saale

Elbe

Halle

Leipzig

Dres

former
East German
border

Erfurt

Gera

Chemnit

Aachen

Bad Hersfeld

THÜRINGEN
FOREST

Zwickau

ERZ MTS.

Bonn

Giessen

Meiningen

Plauen

Koblenz

G E R M A N Y

CZEC
REPUB

Frankfurt-am-Main

Bayreuth

Mainz

Bamberg

Darmstadt

Würzburg

Trier

Mannheim

Ludwigs-hafen

Heidelberg

GERMANY

E U R O P E

Saarbrücke

Heilbronn

Karlsruhe

Stuttgart

Regensburg

BAVARIAN FORE

FRANCE

Ulm

Augsburg

Passa

Munich

Freiburg

Memmingen

Rheinfelden

Ravensburg

L. Constance

Garmisch-
Partenkirchen

Bad
Reichenhall

SWITZERLAND

AUSTRIA

On April 30, 2004, a young computer whiz in Waffensen, Germany, unleashed a worm onto the Internet. This so-called Sasser worm would creep into computers throughout the world.

Worms Crawl In . . .

. . . but they don't crawl out—as Internet users around the world are about to find out.

Somewhere, an evil mastermind was preparing for his ultimate conquest.

He was about to launch an attack on the cyberworld. With just a few keystrokes, he'd created a monster. Well, a worm, actually—a nasty computer program that would crawl throughout the Internet, leaving chaos in its slimy wake.

Deep within his hiding place, the hacker typed in a final command—and brought the computer world to its knees.

So who was this twisted villain? A terrorist plotting a massive attack? A techno-genius planning to steal millions from the world's biggest companies? A revolutionary hoping to bring the government to its knees?

Hardly.

He was a teenage boy sitting at a computer in his basement. People thought of him as a shy and friendly kid. The police later described him as a "geek." It was his 18th birthday. And he had just triggered one of

A hacker slept here. This is the home of Sven Jaschan, creator of the Sasser worm.

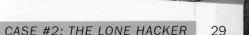

Sasser affected airlines and many other businesses, making it hard for them to serve their clients.

the most destructive cyberattacks ever.

His motive wasn't to cause chaos. Or to make millions. Or even to hurt a soul. He just wanted to brag to his friends.

It was April 30, 2004. The worm he'd created slithered into the Internet. And traffic on the Web came to a screeching halt.

The computers at Delta Air Lines crashed, forcing it to ground all of its planes.

The British Coast Guard couldn't use its electronic mapping service, and parts of Britain's shores were unguarded.

In France, a news agency suddenly lost communication with its satellite.

In Finland, a bank closed 130 offices when its computers shut down.

All across the world, computers crashed or continuously restarted. Companies couldn't do business. Some hospitals had equipment failure, putting people's lives in danger.

How could a single teenager cause so much trouble around the globe? And how could one computer worm cause so much damage?

Creeping Through the Internet

A computer worm attacks quietly—and spreads quickly.

The teenager's name was Sven Jaschan. And his worm became known as the Sasser worm.

Like other worms, Sasser was a computer program that slithered unseen through computer networks. Most worms don't destroy people's files. They usually slow computers down and cause traffic jams on the Internet.

They also spread easily. A virus has to be attached to an e-mail or spread through a file-sharing program. And computer users only catch the virus if they open the infected e-mail or file. But a worm can invade computers directly from the Internet. It doesn't need anyone to open the door. It enters computers on its own.

As a worm roams through the Internet, it's constantly looking for computers to infect. It's programmed to attack computers with operating systems that have flaws in them. Those holes leave the computers open to attack.

According to accounts, Sven Jaschan was egged on by his friends.

When a worm finds a computer with a flawed operating system, it makes a copy of itself. Then it wriggles into its new home.

The Sasser worm attacked the most

popular types of Microsoft operating systems. It affected hundreds of thousands of home and business computers. It caused some to slow down. Others constantly shut down and **rebooted**.

As the Sasser worm traveled, it made copies of itself. Those copies rapidly spread throughout the Internet.

Too Late to Patch

A team of experts at Microsoft are working as quickly as possible. But that isn't fast enough.

Months before Sasser struck, experts at Microsoft realized they had a problem.

They had discovered a hole in two of their operating systems. They knew that worms could attack these systems at any time. To keep worms out, the holes had to be fixed with a **patch**. A patch is new computer **code** that fixes the problems in the original **software**.

An expert team of programmers began working furiously on a patch.

But thousands of miles away, in Waffensen, Germany, Sven Jaschan beat them. On April 30, he released the worm.

Any computer connected to the Web and running the Microsoft software was in danger. That meant there were hundreds of thousands of potential targets for the Sasser worm.

A Microsoft Windows user downloads a patch to protect his computer from the Blaster Worm in 2003. Microsoft also released a patch for the Sasser worm in 2004. But for many users, it was too late.

When Microsoft found out about the worm, the expert team went into high alert. "It became a 24-7 operation," one team member said. "We set up war rooms and went into combat mode."

Within 24 hours, Microsoft had launched a campaign to make people aware of the danger. They posted information about the patch on their Web site. In the next two days, almost 1.5 million people downloaded free Microsoft tools to kill Sasser.

But the damage was already done. Reports of Sasser's impact came from everywhere. The Sasser worm caused computers at many big companies to crash. Computers in half of Taiwan's post offices were infected. The worm hit government offices in Hong Kong and oil platforms in the Gulf of Mexico. American Express lost Internet access for hours.

Sven Jaschan bragged about the worm to his friends. He even showed them the code he wrote to create the worm.

The Worm Turns

A friend turns Sven in—for a big reward.

Back in Germany, Sven was bragging. He told his friends that he was the inventor of the world-famous worm. He showed them lines of code to prove that Sasser was his creation.

Meanwhile, Microsoft and the FBI were searching for the hacker. They studied the worm's code for clues that would help them track it back to its source. It might have taken them months, or even years, to find Sven that way. But then the investigators got a break.

Just five days after the worm appeared, Microsoft's German offices got a call. It was from one of Sven's buddies. He said he would turn in Sasser's creator for $250,000. To prove he meant business, he gave them the section of code Sven had shown him.

Two days later, Sven was sitting at his computer when he heard a banging at his door. Suddenly, the German police burst into his home. They arrested him at gunpoint and confiscated his computer. As his parents watched in shock, Sven was taken to jail.

Sasser was a costly prank. Companies lost money when their computers went down. And some of the problems were expensive to repair. But the experts at Microsoft learned a lot from the experience. They made improvements to their software and patching systems. As a result, it would be much harder today for a lone hacker to do what Sven did in 2004.

Microsoft's reward money made it possible to catch Sven. But it may have made it harder to catch other hackers. They know there's a reward for anyone who turns them in. So they're much slyer. They cover their tracks better. And when they attack, people rarely know it.

Sven Jaschan leaving a court in Verden, Germany, in July 2005. He confessed to creating the Sasser worm.

Newer worms and viruses don't shut computers down. They hide inside hard drives and do their dirty work in secret." [Hackers] have gone underground. They're more professional, more silent," says Andy Jaquith, an analyst an online security company. "Sven is probably the last amateur we'll see."

Sven got lucky. The German courts tried him as a minor. He'd created the worm before his 18th birthday. So instead of serving jail time, he received a 21-month suspended sentence. That means he didn't have to go to prison. He was on probation for three years. And he had to serve 30 hours of community service.

Sven is also being sued for millions of dollars by the companies whose computers were infected.

"It's remarkable . . . that one kid could set the world on its head," says Jaquith. "It shows that a kid with computer smarts—but obviously not world smarts—can cause a lot of trouble." 24/7

Brad Smith was senior vice president at Microsoft in 2004. After Sven was arrested, Smith announced that the company's anti-virus reward program helped German police track down the hacker.

In the next case, a woman monitors terrorist Web sites—to find out what they're planning.

A City in the Northeast
of the U.S.
1990s-present

The Terrorist Hunter

Rita Katz spies on terrorists in
one of their favorite hiding
places—the Internet.

Spying on Terrorists

She's a small woman who spends her days online. So why do terrorists fear her?

Her office is in a Northeastern city. That's all we can tell you. Everything else about it is a secret. Only a handful of people know its location. Even if you got hold of the address, you still might not find her. There's lots of security. She's not listed in the directory in the lobby. And the company name on the door of the office is a fake.

If you did get inside the office (fat chance!), you'd see young people huddled over computers. They're chattering in English, French, and Arabic. Dozens of **mug shots**

Rita Katz was born in Basra, Iraq, in 1963. When she was a young girl, she and her family escaped to Tel Aviv, Israel. She then moved to Washington, D.C. Now that she monitors terrorists online, few people know where she lives.

NORTH
AMERICA

N
W   E
S

ED
S   Washington, D.C.

ATLANTIC
OCEAN

Tel Aviv,
Israel

Basra,
Iraq

ASIA

AFRICA

SOUTH
AMERICA

line the walls. The men in the photos are among the most dangerous people in the world.

And the woman who runs the office is out to get them.

Her name is Rita Katz. She's a mother of four. She is tiny and wears glasses. Katz doesn't fit anyone's image of what a terrorist hunter should look like. But that's what she is.

As a child, Rita Katz and her family escaped from Saddam Hussein's Iraq. She now heads an organization call the SITE Institute, which monitors terrorists online.

Her company is called the SITE Institute. SITE stands for Search for International Terrorist Entities. And that's what Katz does every day—she searches for terrorists who are active on the Web. She then sells any information she comes up with to a client list that includes government agencies and private companies.

Katz and her staff scan the Internet for clues about terrorist plots. They comb through message boards that might have information about future attacks. They sneak into the chat rooms terrorists use to recruit others to their cause. They even pose as terrorists so the bad guys will trust them.

"There is a real war going on in cyberspace, but it is invisible to most of us," says Gabriel Weimann. He's a cyberterrorism expert at the United States Institute of Peace.

That war isn't invisible to Katz. She and her team—made up of translators, terrorism experts, and college interns—spy on terrorists every day. Their job is to keep their eyes open and learn as much as they can. Then they tell government authorities what they found out. That information helps prevent attacks.

How does someone become a terrorist hunter? For Katz, the journey began when she was a kid, growing up in a country ruled by terror.

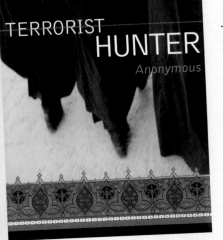

The Extraordinary Story of a Woman Who Went Undercover to Infiltrate the Radical Islamic Groups Operating in America

TERRORIST HUNTER

Anonymous

Rita Katz published a book anonymously in 2003. The book's title is *Terrorist Hunter: The Extraordinary Story of a Woman Who Went Undercover to Infiltrate the Radical Islamic Groups Operating in America.*

A Daring Escape

**Katz's father was killed
by one of the worst dictators in recent history.**

Rita Katz was born in Iraq in 1963. She was one of four children in a wealthy Jewish family. In 1968, Iraqi dictator Saddam Hussein ordered his troops to imprison prominent Iraqi Jews. Rita's father was taken away. The rest of the family was kept under house arrest in a stone hut.

A year later, Rita's father was hanged in the middle of Baghdad's central square. A mob of thousands cheered as he was executed. Rita was just six years old.

Rita's family escaped from their home after her mother drugged the guards. Her mother then posed as the wife of a Iraqi general to sneak the family out of Iraq. The family fled to Israel and settled in a small town by the sea.

Saddam Hussein (*above*) took part in overthrowing the government in Iraq in 1968. In the photo to the left, Hussein is near the microphone, speaking to a crowd after the hanging of 14 Iraqi Jews.

Katz studied history at Tel Aviv University and married a medical student. In 1997, her husband was offered a job in the United States. The couple moved to Washington, D.C. They have four children.

Katz was often homesick. For a while she worked in a gift shop. Then one day, she saw an ad in the paper that changed her life. A group that tracked terrorists over the Internet was looking for an Arabic-speaking research assistant. Katz got the job.

Katz's job was to sneak into terrorists' chat rooms and Web sites. She found and translated messages that might contain clues about terrorists' plans. She also searched for information on the people who gave them money. She knew that a good way to stop the terrorists was to cut off the flow of money.

Katz eventually formed her own team of cyberspies, the SITE Institute. She and her employees spend their days poking around in the Internet's dark corners, searching for clues about terrorist plots.

Scary Sites

Katz's job can be frightening. But she has no plans to quit.

Employees at the SITE Institute visit terrifying sites every day. They read terrorists' blogs that brag about deadly attacks. They watch videos of suicide bombers strapping on explosives. They listen in on hate-filled rants in chat rooms.

Many sites are fakes. Some are just posted by people with hateful opinions. Katz and her staff must weed out the real threats from the pretend ones. Some experts say she gives too much attention to people who are just mouthing off on the Web. They say that since she has no training as a spy, she can't always tell if threats are real or not.

Still, Katz knows her work saves lives. Once, a member of her team used a false identity to join a terrorist chat room. Suicide bombers sometimes went there to post their "wills"—last messages to their friends and families. One day he saw that someone had

Katz looks over a Web site in her office on August 30, 2004, in an undisclosed location.

just posted his will. He knew the suicide bomber was preparing to carry out an attack.

Katz called a **counterintelligence** official she knew in the bomber's country. Within 24 hours, the bomber was under **surveillance**. A week later, he was arrested. Nobody will ever know how many lives were saved that day. In an interview with the *New Yorker* magazine, the official gave Katz all the credit. "[Investigators] probably wouldn't have had a clue if it hadn't been for Rita," he said.

Terrorists know that Katz is spying on them. She sometimes fears for her life. So she never gives out information about her family or her company. She wears a false nose and wig when she appears on TV. But she has no plans to quit. She keeps her laptop nearby when she's making dinner. And she logs on first thing every morning. The bad guys never rest, she says. So the good guys must always be ready. 24/7

CYBERCRIME
DOWNLOAD

Cybercrooks keep coming up with new ways to spy on and steal from people. Here's more information about their scams.

IN THIS SECTION:

- ▶ the history of hacking;
- ▶ how a group tried to kidnap a Web site;
- ▶ phishy e-mails and zombie computers;
- ▶ and whether you might have a career in cybersecurity.

1960s and 1970s **Phrackers**

The **World Wide Web** doesn't yet exist. But hackers are busy breaking into phone networks so they can make free long distance calls. They also misdirect other people's calls. These phone hackers become known as "phrackers" or "phreaks."

1982 **An Early Virus**

One of the first viruses is created by a teenager, who puts it in a computer game. When somebody plays the game for the 50th time, the virus infects the computer. Elk Cloner, as it is called, displays a little rhyme on the screen: "It will get on all your disks / It will infiltrate your chips / Yes, it's Cloner!"

Key Dates in Hacker History

Troublemakers have been creating nasty invaders ever since the early days of the Internet.

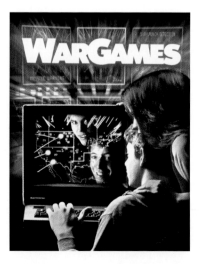

1983 **Fear of Hackers**

The movie *WarGames* makes the public aware of computer hackers. In it, a teenager hacks into a military network as a prank. But he messes up and almost launches nuclear missiles at the Soviet Union. As a result, some people begin worrying that hackers could set off World War III.

1988 An Early Worm

College student Robert Morris (*left*) releases one of the first worms. He just wants to test its effects, but it spreads quicker and farther than Morris expects. It crashes thousands of computers and gets him arrested and kicked out of college.

1989 Cyber Spies Caught

Hackers in West Germany steal information from U.S. government and corporate computers. Then they sell it to the Soviet Union. It's one of the first cyberspy cases to make headlines.

1995 A Big Heist

A Russian group hacks into Citibank accounts and steals $10 million. The ringleader uses his laptop at work to send the money to accounts in other countries. He is caught, and most of the money is recovered.

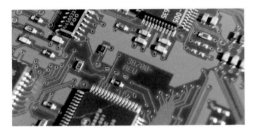

1995 Year of the Hacker

Hackers break into high-security computers at military bases and government agencies. A group called the Internet Liberation Front attacks IBM and other big companies on Thanksgiving. Computer experts realize they have to develop better security systems.

1999 No Joke

Melissa becomes one of the first major worms that travels by e-mail. It burrows into the victim's address book and sends copies of itself to the first 50 contacts. It also inserts quotes from *The Simpsons* into documents. Users don't find it funny.

2004 Sasser Strikes

Sven Jaschan unleashes the Sasser worm, causing chaos in computer networks around the world.

See Case #2.

In the News

Read all about it. Hackers are front-page news!

Hackers Demand Ransom for Kidnapped Web Site

WILTSHIRE, ENGLAND—January 2006

In January 2006, 21-year-old Alex Tew got an e-mail demanding a $50,000 ransom payment. It wasn't for a kidnapped family member. It was for his Web site, the Million Dollar Homepage. It had been taken hostage by hackers who called themselves "The Dark Group." They flooded his site with so much fake traffic that it stopped working. "If you want the site back online, pay $50,000," said the hackers' e-mail.

"I had no intention of paying them," says Tew. Instead, he paid computer security experts thousands of dollars to get his site up and running again. He was able to afford it because he'd made a lot of money

by selling advertising space on his site. He created the site to raise money to go to college. It took him only four months to reach his target of a million dollars.

Security investigators say there has been a rise in hackers as blackmailers. "[Hackers] used to be teenagers looking for bragging rights," says Johannes Ullrichfrom the SANS Institute, a security think tank. "Now it's done for profit."

Alex Tew's Web site made enough money to pay for his college education.

Virtual Robbers Turn Themselves In

BATON ROUGE, LOUISIANA—December 2006

Jim Stickley and Dayle Asbury entered the financial company wearing fire inspector uniforms. They flashed their badges, and the guard waved them in.

Within half an hour, the two had broken into the company's computer network. They now had access to its customer data, which is worth a lot of money. But instead of stealing it, they turned themselves in.

Why? Because they're not really thieves. Stickley is a co-founder of TraceSecurity, a group of sneakers who test companies' security systems. His job is to find their weak spots and help them improve their protection.

In the past four years, TraceSecurity has been hired by many companies, including banks. It managed to break into all their computer networks.

That's scary for consumers, who assume that their personal information is safe with trusted institutions like banks.

Clearly it isn't safe enough. But now companies can hire phony thieves like Stickley to help them. Some security experts were once Black Hats involved in illegal hacking. But now they're White Hats, making cyberspace a safer place.

Sneakers like Jim Stickley reveal weaknesses in computer systems so that companies can make them more secure.

Rough Waters

Danger! The waters of the Internet are filled with sharks. And every day they come up with new ways to sink their teeth into your money. Here are some of their scams.

PHISHING

If something smells phishy, it's probably rotten.

An e-mail arrives offering you a cool new cell phone. Or maybe it's an invitation to join a new friends network. An offer even may look like it comes from a company you know. Clicking on the link takes you to a Web site. There, you're asked for your name, address, phone number, and maybe even a credit card number.

Beware. Crooks are going phishing. They've baited the hook and are waiting for you to bite.

Phishing scams are the biggest schemes on the Net. Some phishers pretend to work for a bank. They claim that the bank needs to update its client information. Or they might pretend to work for a job service. Their e-mail asks people to send their resumes.

Don't be a sucker.

Suckers who give out their personal data are sunk. Phishers can steal from their victims' bank accounts, use their credit cards, or even sell their identities to other people.

Millions of people are tricked every year. About one in six phishing e-mails is opened. And phishing scams pull in more than $2 billion a year for the criminals who run them.

ZOMBIES

Zombies are everywhere. They lurk in people's homes. Run for your life!

This isn't the plot of a horror movie. It's actually happening—inside computers. Thousands of computers have been kidnapped and turned into zombies.

Cybercrooks have programs that allow them to gain control over other people's computers. The send out worms or viruses that turn computers into zombies. Now the bad guys control those computers. They can use them for phishing trips or to send out junk e-mail. The authorities can't trace any illegal activities back to the bad guys' computers.

Watch for warning signs.

People often don't realize their computer has turned into a zombie. It may just slow down, or act strangely. They have no idea that they're harboring criminals in their home.

DON'T GET SCAMMED!

There are plenty of ways you can protect yourself and your computer. Here are some tips.

Don't talk to strangers.

Never reply to any e-mails or pop-up messages that ask for personal information such as passwords or credit card numbers. Phishers try to make e-mails look like they're from a well-known company. But real companies never ask for this kind of information in an e-mail. And be careful not to click on any links in suspicious e-mails.

If it sounds too good to be true, it probably is.

Don't be fooled by e-mails offering free products or money. There aren't any rich strangers out there who want to send you cash. But there are plenty of crooks who use big promises to get hold of people's bank account numbers. And beware of pop-up ads for free downloadable software. They're probably trying to trick you into downloading a virus.

Lock up your valuables.

Crooks try to hack into your computer so they can steal your identity. Protect yourself by installing strong firewalls and anti-virus software. Be sure to update it regularly. Make life hard for scammers so they'll move on to easier targets.

HELP WANTED:
Computer Security Specialist

Do you have what it takes to fight cybercrime? Here's more information about the field.

Ken Dunham works for VeriSign-iDefense, an Internet security company. He leads their Rapid Response Team, which helps track online threats.

Q&A: KEN DUNHAM

24/7: What does an Internet security company like VeriSign-iDefense do?

KEN DUNHAM: A lot of things. Every time you try to go on a dot com, we make sure you get there safely. We [make sure] you are at less risk when you use a credit card online. And we make sure no one hacks into the voting on *American Idol* and other TV shows.

We also work on terrorism issues. It's our job to know what the online bad guys are doing. So we deal with threats—whether it's kids playing online or the Russian mob or terrorists.

24/7: Can the Internet ever really be completely safe?

DUNHAM: We can help keep it *safer*. Today's bad guys aren't kids playing around. Organized criminals are doing most of the attacks. These guys have their hands in just about everything, from viruses to phishing to spam. They are making millions of dollars each year on Internet crime. They're growing very fast. Their technology is shooting through the roof.

24/7: What happens when a cyberattack hits, say, a major company?

DUNHAM: We call that a meltdown. Our clients include 18 of the top 20 financial companies in the world. When they get hit with a virus, they need answers within about three hours.

24/7: Were you always a computer kid?

DUNHAM: I didn't really get deep into computers until college. I bought my own Mac and started getting on the Internet. I remember buying a one-inch-thick (2.5-cm) document that told me how to get on the Internet. I spent two weeks in the library trying to figure out how to get online.

24/7: Do you have to be a computer geek to succeed in Internet security?

DUNHAM: In today's world, everyone has to know some basic computer skills, no matter what job you have. But computer security experts need to be the best of the best.

24/7: What kind of people do you hire?

DUNHAM: We want really smart people who can perform. Many have graduate degrees in computer science. They have great GPAs, and good people skills, they can write effectively, and they are team players. But we also want people who are more than just book smart. We like people who have done something in the real world.

24/7: Does being a gamer help?

DUNHAM: I don't play games. I find them to be a tremendous waste of time and productivity.

24/7: What advice would you give kids who want to get into computer security?

DUNHAM: You need to be the best of the best. You have to work hard, you have to be fully committed, and you have to be single-minded about your career. You need to show a passion. You must love what you do and show your talent.

DO YOU HAVE WHAT IT TAKES?

Take this totally unscientific quiz to see if see if a job protecting the Internet might be a good career choice for you.

1 **Are you good at learning new stuff on the computer?**
- **a)** Yes. I know more about the computer than anyone I know.
- **b)** I'm good enough.
- **c)** If it takes more than five minutes to figure out, I call my little brother.

2 **Do you consider yourself an honest person?**
- **a)** I think that honesty is the most important quality in a person.
- **b)** I believe in being honest, but I think that sometimes you might have to cut some corners.
- **a)** I've got to be honest here. No.

3 **Are you good spy material?**
- **a)** I can keep a secret forever, and I notice everything.
- **b)** I'm pretty observant, but sometimes I do let secrets slip out.
- **c)** I tell my friends everything. And I'm usually lost in my own thoughts.

4 **Are you good at solving problems?**
- **a)** I'm always figuring out new ways to do things.
- **b)** I'm pretty good if I have enough time.
- **c)** I'm good at finding the TV remote. Does that count?

5 **Can you pretend to be someone else?**
- **a)** I can create entirely different personalities.
- **b)** I like to act in plays and really get into being another character.
- **c)** I'm just me, and I can't hide it.

YOUR SCORE

Give yourself 3 points for every "a" you chose. Give yourself 2 points for every "b" you chose. Give yourself 1 point for every "c" you chose.

If you got **13–15 points**, you're a born cybercrime fighter.

If you got **10–12 points**, fighting cybercriminals is a career option.

If you got **5–9 points**, you might want to look at another career.

HOW TO GET STARTED... NOW!

GET AN EDUCATION

▶ Focus on behavior science classes (like psychology and sociology) and computer science.

▶ Start thinking about college. While degress are not necessary for most certification programs, employers do prefer them. Look for universities that offer courses in computer security.

▶ Read the newspaper and go online. Keep up with what's going on in the world. Keep an eye out for articles about online security.

▶ Read anything you can find about computers, security, and psychology.

▶ See the books and Web sites in the Resources section on pages 56–58.

▶ Graduate from high school!

NETWORK!

Go online and do research on local security experts. See if one may be willing to give you advice.

GET AN INTERNSHIP

Look for an internship with a local security expert or information technology (IT) office. Most

It's never too early to start working toward your goals.

companies—both large and small— have IT divisions. More and more have security specialists on staff, too. Call them up and ask for advice or volunteer your services. Sometimes the best way to learn is to observe.

LEARN ABOUT OTHER JOBS IN THE FIELD!

IT positions all tie into one another. Security experts often work with—and in many cases once held—other jobs in computer support.

Some security-related IT fields and positions are: security design, virtual private network implementation, security operations, network architect/ design consultant, network engineer, systems engineer, or network operations.

And that's just a small sampling. This is a line of work that keeps growing every day.

Resources

Looking for more information about cybercrime? Here are some resources you don't want to miss!

PROFESSIONAL ORGANIZATIONS

Central Intelligence Agency (CIA)
www.cia.gov
Office of Public Affairs
Washington, DC 20505
PHONE: 703-482-0623
FAX: 703-482-1739

The CIA was created in 1947 when President Harry Truman signed the National Security Act. The organization works to collect information that will help keep the United States safe. It also engages in research and development of high-level technology for gathering intelligence around the world.

Federal Bureau of Investigation (FBI)
www.fbi.gov
J. Edgar Hoover Building
935 Pennsylvania Avenue, NW
Washington, DC 20535
PHONE: 202-324-3000

The FBI works to protect and defend the United States from terrorism and foreign threats. It also upholds the criminal laws of the United States and provides leadership for federal, state, and local law enforcement.

U.S. Department of Homeland Security (DHS)
www.dhs.gov
Washington, DC 20528
PHONE: 202-282-8000

This department was created in 2002 to protect the United States from terrorist attacks.

U.S. Department of Justice
www.cybercrime.gov
10th & Constitution Avenue, NW
Criminal Division (CCIPS)
John C. Keeney Building, Suite 600
Washington, DC 20530
PHONE: 202-514-2007

The Computer Crime and Intellectual Property Section (CCIPS) is part of the U.S. Department of Justice. It is responsible for implementing national strategies in combating computer and intellectual property crimes worldwide.

U.S. Department of State
www.state.gov
2201 C Street, NW
Washington, DC 20520
PHONE: 202-647-4000

The mission of the U.S. State Department is to create a more secure, democratic, and prosperous world for people in the United States and the international community. The people of the State Department use diplomacy, negotiation, and intelligence to work with other countries throughout the world.

WEB SITES

Center for Internet Security
www.cisecruity.org

This site is run by a nonprofit organization that helps businesses keep their computer systems safe.

CERT
www.cert.org

Learn more about CERT, part of the Software Engineering Institute (SEI), a federally funded research and development center at Carnegie Mellon University in Pittsburgh, Pennsylvania.

Crime Library
www.crimelibrary.com/terrorists_spies/spies/index.html

This section of the crime library has true stories about terrorists, spies, and assassins.

Cybercrime Law
www.cybercrimelaw.org

This is a weblog that focuses on detecting and preventing online crime.

Cyber Criminals Most Wanted
www.ccmostwanted.com/

Check out cyber safety issues all over the world.

Department of Defense Cyber Crime Center
www.dc3.mil/dc3/home.htm

This center was created in October 2001 to combat cybercrime that affects the Department of Defense.

Take a Bite Out of Cyber Crime
www.bytecrime.org/

McGruff the Crime Dog teaches kids and families how to keep themselves safe online.

BOOKS

Bauchner, Elizabeth. *Computer Investigation* (Forensics: The Science of Crime-Solving). Broomall, Pa.: Mason Crest Publishers, 2005.

Brequet, Teri. *Frequently Asked Questions About Cyberbullying.* New York: Rosen Publishing, 2007.

Grant-Adamson, Andrew. *Cyber Crime* (Crime and Detection). Broomall, Pa.: Mason Crest Publishers, 2002.

Judson, Karen. *Computer Crime: Phreaks, Spies and Salami Slicers.* Berkeley Heights, N.J.: Enslow Publishers, 2000.

Knittel, John. *Everything You Need to Know About the Dangers of Computer Hacking.* New York: Rosen Publishing, 2000.

Platt, Richard, and John Townsend. *Cyber Crime* (Freestyle, True Crime). Austin: Raintree Publishers, 2004.

Sherman, Jopsepha. *Internet Security* (Watts Library). Danbury, Conn.: Franklin Watts, 2003.

Wolinksy, Art. *Safe Surfing on the Internet.* Berkeley Heights, N.J.: Enslow Publishers, 2003.

A

Al Qaeda (al KYE-dah) *noun* an Islamic terrorist group that is well known for attacking the United States on September 11, 2001. It was established in 1988 by Osama bin Laden.

B

Black Hats (blak hats) *noun* dangerous hackers who try to break into computer systems

C

CIA (see-eye-AY) *noun* an agency of the U.S. government that deals with foreign intelligence (the secrets and knowledge of other countries) and counterintelligence (misleading spies from other countries). It stands for *Central Intelligence Agency*.

code (kode) *noun* a set of instructions for a computer

counterintelligence (kown-tur-in-TEL-uh-juhnss) *noun* information used to mislead spies from other countries

crash (krash) *verb* to suffer a major failure, usually with a loss of data

cyberattack (SYE-bur-uh-tak) *noun* a destructive act against a computer system

cyberterrorism (SYE-bur-TAIR-ur-izm) *noun* a major attack on the computer networks that control power grids and other large systems

D

DHS (DEE-aych-ess) *noun* a U.S. government agency that was created to protect the country from terrorists. It stands for *Department of Homeland Security*.

downloaded (DOWN-lode-ed) *verb* transferred data or files from one place (a larger computer, a Web site, an e-mail, etc.) to a computer

E

expertise (ex-pur-TEEZ) *noun* the skill of an expert

Dictionary

F

FBI (eff-bee-EYE) *noun* a U.S. government agency that fights terrorism and organized crime. It stands for the *Federal Bureau of Investigation*.

firewall (FYRE-wahl) *noun* an electronic barrier that keeps out hackers

H

hacker (HAK-ur) *noun* a highly skilled programmer who uses his or her skills to break into computer networks

honeypots (HUN-ee-pots) *noun* traps set by White Hats to catch Black Hats

I

identity thieves (eye-DEN-tuh-tee theevz) *noun* people who steal Social Security numbers, credit card numbers, and other personal information

infrastructure (in-frah-STRUK-shur) *noun* the basic systems serving an area—like transportation and communication systems, power plants, and schools

M

mug shots (mug shots) *noun* photos of people who are wanted for committing crimes

P

patch (patch) *noun* a new computer code created to fix problems in the original software

phishing (FISH-ing) *noun* a computer scam that involves sending out spam that looks real; phishers trick computer users into giving them their personal information

R

rebooted (ree-BOOT-ed) *verb* turned on again

S

scenarios (suh-NAIR-ee-ohz) *noun* possible series of events

script kiddie (skript KID-ee) *noun* an inexperienced or unskilled hacker who uses programs written by someone else to break into computer systems

sneakers (SNEE-kurz) *noun* hackers who are hired by companies to check the security of their Web sites and security systems

Social Security (SOH-shul suh-KYUR-uh-tee) *noun* a U.S. government program that provides funds for retired citizens; people are assigned Social Security numbers as a means of identification.

software (SAWFT-wair) *noun* programs used on a computer system

spam (spam) *noun* unwanted e-mail sent to a large number of people

surveillance (sur-VAY-luhnss) *noun* close watch of something or someone

T

tapped (tapt) *verb* cut in on telephone lines or radio signals to get information

terrorist (TAIR-ur-ist) *noun* a person who tries to control other people through violence, usually for political reasons

tiger teams (TYE-gur teemz) *noun* groups of sneakers, people who are hired to test companies' security systems

Trojan horse (TRO-jun hors) *noun* a program that looks like useful software but really contains a virus or other harmful program

V

virus (VYE-rus) *noun* a destructive computer program that enters people's computers without their knowledge

W

White Hats (whyte hats) *noun* people who work to stop Black Hats (computer hackers) and make cyberspace safe

World Wide Web (wurld wyde web) *noun* a network-based system for browsing Internet sites; often called the Web

worm (wurm) *noun* a nasty program that slows or shuts down computers

Z

zombies (ZOM-beez) *noun* computers that have been taken over by hackers using a program called a bot

Index

What I find interesting about hackers and the security experts who try to outsmart them is that they are alike. They work on different sides of the law, but you get the feeling that the bad guys might make pretty effective good guys if things worked out differently in their lives.

Anyone who has ever had a virus get onto their computer knows the trouble they can cause. The work that computer security people do to fight hackers is very important. Without them, our lives would truly be very different.

CONTENT ADVISER: Sara Sinclair, Dartmouth College PKI/ Trust Laboratory

[Cyber Fact]

Polls show that young Americans don't worry a lot about threats to their computers. About 40 percent of people under 25 think they're more likely to get hit by lightning than have a virus attack their computer. They are so wrong! The odds of being hit by lightning are approximately one in 294,330,406. The odds of ending up on the wrong end of a worm, virus, or phishing attack are seven in ten.